English - Esperanto

By
Gilad Soffer

Table of Contents

numbers

numbers - nombroj

zero - nulo

one - unu

two - du

three - tri

four - kvar

five - kvin

six - ses

eight - ok

nine - naŭ

ten - dek

eleven - dekunu

twelve - dekdu

thirteen - dektri

fourteen - dek kvar

fifteen - dek kvin

twenty - dudek

thirty - tridek

forty - kvardek

fifty - kvindek

sixty - sesdek

seventy - sepdek

eighty - okdek

ninety - naŭdek

hundred - cent

colors

colors - koloroj

red - ruĝa

yellow - flava

orange - oranĝo

blue - blua

white - blanka

gray - grizaj

brown - bruna

black - nigra

time

time - tempo

after - post

afternoon - posttagmezon

afterwards - poste

alarm clock - vekhorloĝo

annual - ĉiujara

anytime - ĉiutempe

before - antaŭ

century - jarcento

clock - horloĝo

day - tagon

daylight - taglumo

decade - jardeko

delay - malfruo

delayed - prokrastita

early - frua

evening - vespero

everyday - ĉiutaga

future - estonteco

hour - horo

late - malfrue

later - poste

leap year - superjaro

midnight - noktomezo

millennium - jarmilo

millisecond - milisegundo

minute - minuto

moment - momenton

momentarily - momente

month - monato

morning - mateno

night - nokto

nighttime - dumnokta

noon - tagmezo

now - nun

on time - ĝustatempe

overtime - kromhorojn

past - estinteco

period - periodo

premature - antaŭtempa

present - ĉeestanta

punctual - akurataj

quarter hour - kvara horo

schedule - horaro

season - sezono

second - dua

semester - semestro

someday - iun tagon

sometime - iam

soon - baldaŭ

stopwatch - cronómetro

sunrise - sunleviĝo

sunset - sunsubiro

synchronized - sinkronigita

then - tiam

time zone - horzono

tonight - ĉinokte

today - hodiaŭ

tomorrow - morgaŭ

twilight - krepusko

watch - spekti

week - semajno

wristwatch - horloĝo

year - jaro

yesterday - hieraŭ

what time is it? - kioma horo estas?

it's one o'clock - ĝi estas unu horo

half past one - duono estinteco

quarter past one - kvarono

days

days - tagoj

monday - lundo

tuesday - mardo

wednesday - merkredo

thursday - ĵaŭdo

friday - vendredo

saturday - sabato

sunday - dimanĉo

body

body - korpo

abdomen - abdomeno

anatomy - anatomio

ankle - maleolo

anus - anuso

appendix - apendicon

arm - brako

back - reen

belly - ventro

belly button - umbiliko

bladder - veziko

blood - sango

blood vessels - angioj

bone - osto

brain - cerbo

breast - brustaĵo

buttocks - lumboj

calf - bovidon

cell - ĉelo

cheek - vango

chest - brusto

chin - mentono

circulatory system - cirkulada sistemo

diaphragm - diafragmo

ear - orelo

ear lobe - orelo lobo

elbow - kubuto

eye - okulo

eyebrow - brovo

eyelashes - okulharoj

eyelid - palpebro

face - vizaĝo

feet - piedojn

finger - fingro

fingernail - ungo

foot - piedo

forehead - frunto

gums - gingivoj

hair - haroj

hand - manoj

head - kapo

heart - koro

body

heel - kalkano

hip - kokso

immune system - imunsistemo

index finger - montrofingro

intestines - intestoj

iris - iridon

jaw - makzelo

kidney - reno

knee - genuo

leg - kruro

lip - lipo

liver - hepato

lobe - lobo

lungs - pulmoj

mouth - bûŝo

muscle - muskolo

nail - najlo

navel - umbiliko

neck - kolo

nerves - nervojn

nipple - cico

nose - nazon

nostril - naztruo

organs - organoj

palm - palmo

pupil - lernanto

rectum - rekta

ribs - ripoj

shoulder - ŝultro

shoulder blade - skapolo

skeleton - skeleto

skin - haŭto

skull - kranio

sole - plando

spinal cord - medolo espinal

spine - vertebraro

stomach - stomako

teeth - dentoj

tendon - tendeno

thigh - femuro

throat - gorĝo

thumb - dikfingro

body

toe - piedfingro

tongue - lingvo

tonsils - tonsiloj

tooth - denton

waist - talio

wrist - pojno

greeting

greeting - saluto

hello - saluton

goodbye - adiaŭ

thanks - dankon

good day - bonan tagon

good night - bonan nokton

how is it going? - kial tuj?

my name is john - mia nomo estas johano

welcome - bonvenon

please - bonvolu

weather

weather - vetero

rainy - pluva

cloudy - nuban

snowy - neĝa

sunny - sunplena

forecast - antaŭvidon

temperature - temperaturo

hot - varmega

warm - varma

cool - malvarmeta

freezing - congelación

foggy - nebula

windy - ventplena

shopping

shopping - komerca

travel agency - vojaĝagentejo

butcher - viandisto

sweet shop - sukeraĵejo

flower shop - florería

gas station - benzinejo

department store - magazenoj

cake shop - kuko vendejo

hairdressers - frizistoj

fish shop - fiŝo vendejo

buy - aĉeti

sell - vendi

price - prezo

how much does it cost? - kiom ĝi kostos?

it costs too much - kostas tro multe

lower the price - malaltigi la prezon

health

health - sano

medicine - medicino

hospital - malsanulejo

pain - doloro

blood - sango

hurt - vundita

it hurts - doloras

to bleed - sangrar

breath - spirado

suffocate - sufoki

doctor - kuracisto

nurse - flegistino

emergency

emergency - kriz

fireman - fajrestingisto

ambulance - ambulanco

police - policano

policeman - policanon

paramedic - paramédico

fire truck - fajro kamiono

ladder - ŝtupetaro

fire escape - fajro eskapo

fire - fajro

thief - ŝtelisto

help - helpi

gun - pafilo

call the police - alvoki policanon

get help - akiri helpon

restaurant

restaurant - restoracio

waitress - kelnerino

cook - kuiristino

table - tablo

check - kontroli

menu - menuo

plate - plato

knife - trancîlo

spoon - kulero

glass - vitro

water - akvo

food

food - manĝaĵo

apple - pomon

apricot - abrikoto

artichoke - artiŝoko

asparagus - asparagoj

ate - manĝis

avocado - avokado

bacon - lardo

banana - banano

basil - bazilio

batter - bateador

beans - faboj

beef - bovaĵo

bitter - maldolĉa

black beans - nigra faboj

blackberry - maŭrino

boil - sxvelajxon

bowl - bovlo

bran - brano

bread - pano

breadfruit - aca

breakfast - matenmanĝo

broccoli - brokolo

broil - boligi

brown rice - bruna rizo

buckwheat - poligona

buns - bulkojn

butter - butero

butter bean - butero fabo

cake - kuko

calorie - kalorio

candy - dolĉaĵoj

carrot - karoto

cashew - anacardo

cheese - fromaĝo

chef - kuiristo

cherry - ĉerizo

chew - maĉi

chicken - kokido

chili - chile

chips - blatoj

chocolate - ĉokolado

chopsticks - palillos

cinnamon - cinamo

coconut - kokoso

coffee - kafo

cook - kuiristino

cookbook - kuirlibro

cookie - kuketo

corn - grajnoj

cornflakes - maizflokoj

cottage cheese - dometo fromaĝo

crab - krabon

cream - kremo

cream cheese - kremo fromaĝo

crust - ŝelo

cucumber - kukumo

cuisine - kuirarto

cupboard - ŝranko

cupcake - magdalena

dates - datoj

dessert - deserton

diet - dieto

dill - aneto

dine - matenmangxi

diner - restoracio

dinner - vespermanĝo

dish - plado

dough - pasto

doughnut - benjeto

dried - sekigitaj

drink - trinkaĵon

dry - seka

eat - manĝi

edible - manĝebla

egg - ovo

eggplant - melongeno

entree - enirpago

fat - graso

feast - festo

fed - nutritaj

fig - figo

fish - fiŝo

flour - faruno

food - nutraĵo

fork - disforkiĝo

freezer - frostujo

fried - fritita

frosting - glazuro

fruit - fruktoj

garlic - ajlo

ginger - zingibro

grape - vinbero

grapefruit - grapfrukto

grated - rallado

gravy - saŭco

herbs - herboj

ham - ŝinko

hamburger - hamburgero

honey - mielo

hot - varmega

hunger - malsato

hungry - malsata

ice - glacio

icing - ĉerizo

ice cream - glaciaĵo

ice cream cone - glaciaĵo konuso

jam - konfitaĵo

jelly - ĵeleo

juice - suko

junk food - manĝita rubo

kebab - kebabo

ketchup - keĉupo

kettle - kaldrono

kitchen - kuirejo

kiwi - kivo

knife - tranĉilo

lamb - ŝafido

lemon - citrono

lettuce - laktuko

lime - kalko

liver - hepato

loaf - panbulo

lobster - omaro

lunch - tagmanĝo

macaroni - makaronio

mango - tenilo

maple syrup - acero siropo

margarine - margarino

marshmallow - melcocha

mashed potatoes - puré terpomoj

mayonnaise - majonezo

meat - viando

meatball - knelo

melon - melono

menu - menuo

meringue - meringo

milk - lakto

milkshake - batita

mint - mento

mints - mentoj

mug - kruĉon

mushroom - fungo

mussels - mituloj

mustard - mustardo

napkin - buŝtuko

nut - nukso

oatmeal - aveno

oil - petrolo

olive - oleastra

onion - cepo

orange - oranĝo

order - ordon

oregano - origano

oven - forno

oyster - ostro

pancake - krespo

papaya - lakteca

pastry - kukvendejo

peach - persiko

peanut - arakido

peanut butter - mani buteron

pea - pizo

pepper - pipro

pickle - pekli

picnic - piknik

pie - kukaĵon

pineapple - ananaso

pita bread - pita pano

pizza - pico

plate - plato

plum - pruno

pomelo - pampelmuso

pork - porkaĵo

pork chops - porkaĵo kotletojn

potato - terpomo

preserves - antaŭgardas

protein - proteinoj

provisions - provizoj

prune - pritrancxu

pudding - pudingo

pumpkin - kukurbo

raspberry - frambo

rations - porcioj

ravioli - raviolo

recipe - recepto

refreshments - malvarmeta

refrigerator - fridujo

ribs - ripoj

rice - rizo

roast - rostita

roll - rulo

salad - salato

salmon - salmo

salsa - saŭco

salt - sala

sandwich - sandviĉo

sauce - saŭco

sausage - kolbaso

savory - bongustan

scallops - veneras

scrambled - kirlitaj

seaweed - algoj

seeds - semoj

sesame seed - sésamo semoj

shrimp - salikoko

slice - tranĉaĵo

smoked - fumaĵita

snack - aperitivo

soda - sodo

sorghum - sorgo

sorrel - brunaj

soup - supo

sour - nematurajn

soy - sojfabo

soybeans - sojfabo

spices - spicoj

spicy - pika

spoon - kulero

sprinkles - aspergas

squid - kalmaro

steak - bifsteko

stew - kuiraĵo

stomach - stomako

stove - forno

straw - pajlo

strawberry - frago

sugar - sukero

sunflower - sunfloro

sushi - suŝion

sweet potato - batato

swiss chard - svisaj chard

syrup - siropo

taco - bilardbastono

tea - teo

teapot - tekruĉo

toast - toasto

tuna - tinuso

turkey - meleagro

vanilla - vanilo

vegetable - vegetaĵa

vinegar - vinagro

vitamin - vitamino

walnut - juglando

water - akvo

watercress - berro

watermelon - akvomelono

wheat - tritiko

whipped cream - skurĝita kremo

yam - ignamo

yeast - feĉo

yogurt - jogurto

yolk - yema

airport

airport - flughaveno

baggage - pakaĵoj

suitcase - valizo

ticket - bileto

security guard - gardisto

metal detector - metalo detektilo

plane - ebeno

flight - fuĝo

relationship

relationship - interrilato

husband - edzo

wife - edzino

son - filo

daughter - filino

brother - fraton

sister - fratino

father - patro

mother - patrino

grandfather - avo

grandmother - avino

aunt - onklino

uncle - onklo

nephew - nevo

niece - nevino

car

car - aŭto

accelerator - akcelilo

airbag - aerkuseno

air conditioner - aero kondiĉita

air conditioning - aero kondiĉita

alarm - alarmo

alternator - alternatoro

antenna - anteno

armrest - reposabrazos

auto - aŭtomata

back-up lights - back-up lumoj

battery - kuirilaro

brake light - dispecigis lumo

brake pedal - dispecigis pedalo

brakes - bremsoj

clutch - ovaro

computer - komputilo

console - konzolo

cooling system - malvarmigo sistemo

cruise control - transepto kontrolo

cylinder - cilindro

dashboard - panelo

diesel engine - diesel

door - pordo

door handle - pordo tenilo

driver's seat - ŝoforo sidloko

emergency brake - kriz dispecigis

emergency lights - kriz lumoj

engine - motoro

exhaust pipe - tubo de ellasilo

exhaust system - ellasilo sistemo

floor mat - planko mato

fog light - nebulo lumo

fuel - brulaĵo

fuse - meĉo

gas - gaso

gas pedal - gaso pedalo

gasoline - benzino

gas tank - kanistron

gearbox - ŝanĝo

gear shift - dentaĵo movo

glove compartment - ganto kupeo

hand brake - mano bremsoj

headlight - lumturoj

hood - kapuĉo

horn - korno

hybrid - híbrido

ignition - sparkado

interior light - interno lumo

key - ŝlosilo

license plate - aŭtokodaj

lights - lumoj

lock - ŝlosi

mat - mato

mirror - spegulo

motor - motoro

navigation system - navigado sistemo

oil - petrolo

oil tank - oleo tank

parking brake - parkado dispecigis

parking lights - parkado lumoj

passenger seat - pasaĝero sidejo

pedal - pedalo

piston - piŝto

radiator - radiatoro

rear-view mirror - retrospegulo

reverse light - dorsflanko lumo

roof - tegmento

seat - seĝo

seat belt - sidejo rimeno

shift - ŝanĝo

shock absorber - skusorbilo

side airbags - flanko aerkusenoj

side mirror - flanko spegulo

spare tire - rezervaj pneŭo

spark plug - sparkilo

speaker - parolanto

speedometer - rapidometro

starter - malfermilo

steering wheel - stirrado

sunroof - plafono

tire - pneŭo

transmission - transdono

trunk - trunko

turn signal - turni signalon

warning light - averto lumo

wheel - radon

window - fenestro

windshield - ekrano

windshield wiper - viŝilo

good - bonaj

friendly - amika

sensitive - sentemaj

loving - ama

cheerful - ĝoja

clever - saĝa

shy - timida

serious - serioza

polite - gxentila

punctual - akurataj

active - aktiva

witty - spritaj

smart - inteligenta

bad - malbona

stupid - malsaĝa

furious - furioza

boring - enuiga

crude - kruda

strict - strikta

hostile - malfavora

cowardly - malkuraĝa

arrogant - aroganta

intolerable - netolerebla

greedy - manĝegema

positive feelings

positive feelings - pozitiva sentoj

happy - feliĉa

joy - ĝojo

to be happy - esti feliĉa

contented - kontenta

calm - trankvila

affection - korinklinon

to like - ŝati

to desire - deziri

happiness - feliĉo

negative feelings

negative feelings - negativa sentoj

sad - malĝoja

sadness - malgajo

to cry - plori

tear - disŝiri

shame - hontigi

to become angry - fariĝi kolera

angry - kolera

to become bored - tedi

worried - maltrankviligita

nervous - nerva

envy - envio

envious - envia

fear - timo

beach

beach - plaĝo

bathing suit - bañador

bay - golfeto

beach - plaĝo

bikini - bikino

boat - kruĉo

clam - mitulo

coast - marbordo

cooler - malvarmeta

coral - korala

crab - krabon

currents - fluoj

dock - doko

dune - duno

dune buggy - duno kalesxo

fins - naĝiloj

fish - fiŝo

fishing - fiŝkaptado

hat - ĉapelo

hermit crab - ermito krabo

high tide - alta tajdo

ice cream - glaciaĵo

intertidal zone - intertidal zono

island - insulo

jellyfish - meduzoj

kayak - kajako

lagoon - lageto

lake - lago

life jacket - savzono

life preserver - vivo savanto

low tide - malalta tajdo

ocean - oceano

palm tree - palmo

reef - rifon

relax - malstreĉiĝi

rest - resto

rip current - rip aktuala

sail - velo

sailboat - velŝipo

salt water - sala akvo

sand - sablon

sandals - sandalojn

sea - maro

seagull - mevo

seashore - bordo

sea star - maro stelo

shark - ŝarko

shell - konko

ship - ŝipo

shore - bordo

shorebirds - vadbirdoj

snacks - manĝetoj

sun - suno

sunbathe - sunumi

sunburn - sunŝirman

sunglasses - sunvitroj

beach

sun hat - suno ĉapelo

surfboard - tabulo de surf

swim - naĝi

swim fins - naĝi naĝiloj

swimming cap - naĝado ĉapo

tide - tajdo

tide pool - tajdo pool

towel - tuko

umbrella - ombrelo

undertow - subfluo

underwater - subakva

vacation - ferioj

volleyball - voleibol

water - akvo

water bottle - akvo botelo

waves - ondoj

wet - malseka

wharf - risorto

yacht - jaĥto

bus - aŭtobuso

taxi - taksio

train - trajno

airplane - aviadilo

subway - metroo

streetcar - tramo

conductor - konduktoro

platform - kajo

turnstile - _turnstile_

engineer - inĝeniero

sports

sports - sportoj

athlete - sportisto

sport - sporto

player - ludanto

team - teamo

training - trejnado

game - ludo

competition - konkurado

championship - konkurso

champion - ĉampiono

record - rekordo

to win - gajni

to lose - perdi

bathroom

bathroom - banĉambro

bathtub - banujo

toilet - necesejo

sink - profundiĝi

medicine cabinet - medicino kabineto

water - akvo

soap - sapo

towel - tuko

curtain rod - kurteno vergo

shower cap - duŝo ĉapo

shower - duŝo

soap dish - sapo plado

sponge - spongon

shampoo - ŝampuo

drain - malplenigi

animals

animals - bestoj

alligator - aligatoro

baboon - babuino

bat - vesperto

bear - urso

beaver - kastoro

bee - abelo

butterfly - papilio

camel - kamelo

cat - kato

chicken - kokido

chimpanzee - ĉimpanzo

cow - bovino

crab - krabo

crow - korvo

deer - cervo

dinosaur - dinosaŭra

dog - hundo

dolphin - delfeno

donkey - azeno

duck - anaso

elephant - elefanto

fish - fiŝoj

fox - vulpo

frog - rano

giraffe - ĝirafo

goat - kaprino

hippopotamus - hipopotamo

horse - ĉevalo

kangaroo - kanguruo

monkey - simion

mouse - muso

penguin - pingveno

pig - porko

pigeon - kolombido

rabbit - kuniklo

shark - ŝarko

sheep - ŝafo

snail - limako

snake - serpento

tiger - tigro

turtle - testudo

weasel - mustelo

whale - baleno

wolf - lupo

zebra - zebro

house

house - domo

air conditioner - aero kondiĉita

attic - subtegmento

back door - malantaŭa pordo

basement - kelo

bathroom - banĉambro

bathtub - banujo

bedroom - dormĉambro

blinds - persienoj

broom - balailo

carpet - tapiŝo

ceiling - plafono

cellar - kelo

chimney - kameno

closet - ŝranko

column - kolono

concrete - betono

cupboard - ŝranko

curtains - kurtenoj

dining room - manĝoĉambro

dish washer - plado washer

door - pordo

door bell - pordo sonorilo

doorknob - klinkon

doorway - pordejo

downstairs - teretaĝo

drain - malplenigi

dryer - sekigilo

electrical system - elektra sistemo

entrance - eniro

fan - ventolilo

fence - heĝo

fireplace - kameno

floor - planko

front door - dompordo

furnace - fajrujo

furniture - mebloj

fuse box - fuzo skatolo

garage - garaĝo

garage door - garaĝo pordo

garbage can - rubo tedaĵo

garden - ĝardeno

house

garden shed - ĝardeno ŝedo

gate - pordego

greenhouse - forcejo

hall - salono

hallway - koridoro

home - hejmo

hose - hoso

key - ŝlosilo

kitchen - kuirejo

ladder - ŝtupetaro

lamp - lampo

laundry - lavbutiko

laundry room - lavejo

lawnmower - gazono

library - biblioteko

light - malpeza

living room - salono

lock - ŝlosi

mailbox - poŝtkesto

mantle - mantelo

mat - mato

mirror - spegulo

painting - pentraĵo

patio - korto

picture - foton

plumbing - fontanería

pool - naĝejo

porch - portiko

roof - tegmento

room - ĉambro

rug - tapiŝeto

shed - versxis

shelf - breton

shelves - bretoj

shower - duŝo

shutters - ŝutroj

sink - profundiĝi

staircase - ŝtuparo

storage shed - stokado ŝedo

storm door - ŝtormo pordo

stove - forno

swimming pool - naĝejo

threshhold - sojlo

toilet - necesejo

trash can - trash tedaĵo

tub - tina

upstairs - supre

vacuum cleaner - polvosuĉilo

wall - muro

washing machine - lavmaŝino

waste basket - basurero

water heater - akvo heater

welcome mat - bonvenon mato

window - fenestro

wood stove - ligno forno

yard - jardo

CPSIA information can be obtained
at www.ICGtesting.com
Printed in the USA
LVHW081207041118
595895LV00024B/712/P